Foreword

by Jim Etherington *Bonfire Historian*

When you have lived in Lewes all your life as I have, Bonfire Night takes on a regularity that forms an intrinsic element of the social calendar of the town. It is difficult to find Lewesians who have not themselves, at some time or other, participated in the annual celebration to commemorate the Discovery of the Gunpowder Plot, or have friends or relatives who have done so. Many will proudly admit to life-long membership of one of the Bonfire societies, often recalling how they were carried in the procession in their parents' arms at an early age. The first experience of Bonfire Night for both my own children, like those of many members, was being perambulated around the streets of Lewes in their society's processions. Other Bonfire Boys can boast of membership spanning many years. New members are often introduced to the societies by relatives of friends. They soon realise they have entered a fraternity of Lewesians that is very conscious of tradition, past historical events, and the burning determination to ensure the continuation of a Saturnalia that snubs its nose at any who consider the Lewes celebrations an irritating anachronism that should be terminated.

To really experience the thrill of the night it is essential to become part of it, either as a spectator, or at closer quarters as a participant. What outsiders do [...] for active society members involvement is a year-long commitment, attending regular committee meetings, organising or assisting in fundraising events (the Bonfire Boys go cap in hand to no one!), and enjoying society social events. It is only as the 'Fifth' nears that more members become more actively involved, assisting in the building of firework displays, the making of torches, the selling of programmes and a myriad of other tasks that are essential to make this year's Fifth better than any that has gone before it. Finally, on the night, the mass of general members, resplendent in costumes that have often taken a year to make, take to the streets to provide Lewes with a unique spectacle unsurpassed anywhere else in the country.

In this book, through his atmospheric photographs, Andy truly captures the visual impact of Lewes Bonfire Night that so excites the spectator. His informative text supplements these images by providing the reader with lucid explanations of the spectacle that is observed. Refreshingly, like all good Lewesians, Andy readily expresses his own opinions of recent trends that are impacting on today's celebrations.

Jim is the author of Lewes Bonfire Night *(S B Publications, 1993), the definitive history of the Fifth celebrations in Lewes, and* Bonfire *(S B Publications, 1997), a photographic guide to society activities*

Lewes

Lewes is a picturesque town in the south-east corner of England. Nestled in an East Sussex river valley in the heart of the South Downs, it seems, on the surface, to be a quiet middle-class town, of no great threat to the natural order of things. Yet there is something about this community that always manages to challenge the status quo and go out on a limb for things which others might shy away from.

The origins of settlement at Lewes go back before Roman times. The presence of three huge earthwork mounds (with others having been removed in the last few centuries) and the archaeological finds within them has suggested to some that Lewes (a word at least partly derived from the Old English *hlaewas*, meaning mounds or hills) may once have been a significant centre for Iron Age man, with all the long-established Pagan rituals of the time.

The Lewes we know today, though, was begun by the Anglo-Saxons around 500 AD, and its general layout, poised on a promontory of downs reaching towards the Ouse Valley, has remained. The Norman invasion of 1066 resulted in the impressive castle that towers over the town, and the work of the Norman Earl William de Warrene gave us much of the existing geography of the town centre, and also the impressive Cluniac Priory, now just a ruin.

The battle that took place in fields around Lewes in 1264, which resulted in King Henry III having to make power concessions to the belligerent barons, is precisely the kind of thing Lewes seems to continually attract - challenges to authority. As the eighteenth and nineteenth centuries made Lewes a trendy and architecturally beautiful place to be, so it attracted several names which have tried to awaken new thinking. Its most famous resident, the rights campaigner Thomas Paine, who influenced the French and American revolutions, is the most obvious example, but other local pioneers like Dr Gideon Mantell, who was the first-ever identifier of dinosaur bones, have all in their way upset the old order of things. There are many other examples.

Today, that habit of rocking the boat lives on, with much political and social activism still alive and well in Lewes. The 2008 announcement, which made national news, that Lewes was cheekily setting up its own currency, courtesy of its local 'Transition Town' environmental group, was typical of the daring and trailblazing kind of thing Lewes does well.

However, never is the real face of Lewes more obvious than on the one night of the year where it truly removes its facade of respectability and shows what the 'freedom of the streets' really means - November the Fifth, or 'Bonfire Night'.

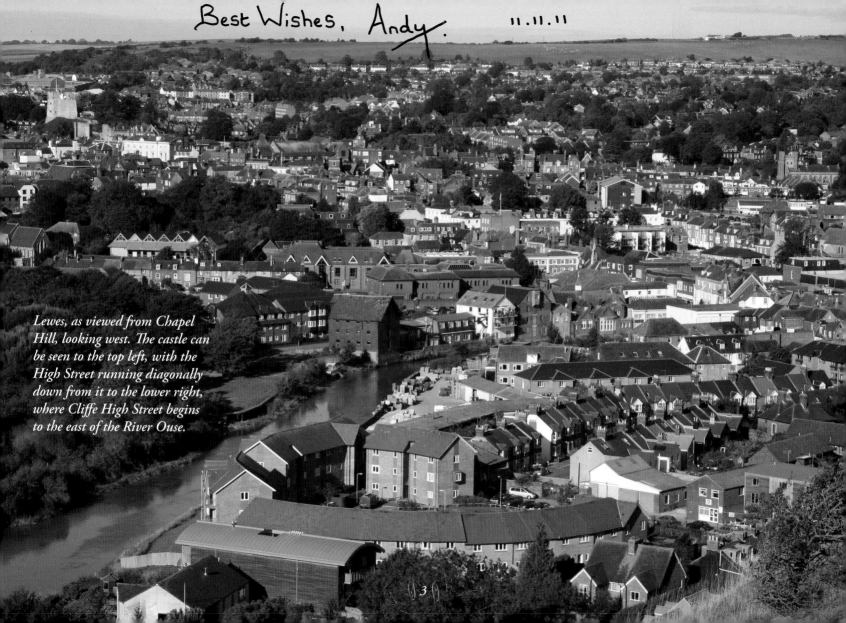

Best Wishes, Andy.   11.11.11

Lewes, as viewed from Chapel Hill, looking west. The castle can be seen to the top left, with the High Street running diagonally down from it to the lower right, where Cliffe High Street begins to the east of the River Ouse.

Bonfire History

When, on 5th November 1605, one Guido Fawkes was caught beneath the then Houses of Parliament, poised to ignite barrels of gunpowder which would have assassinated King James I and his Protestant dignitaries, the revelation of the plot inspired a government Act which proclaimed that the day should be 'held in perpetual remembrance'. Special prayers were to be offered, church bells rung and cannons fired. Essentially an incitement for yet more persecution of Roman Catholicism in England, which had begun with the Reformation and break from Papal rule during Henry VIII's reign, by the eighteenth century the 'Fifth' had become an excuse for rowdy celebrations and mob-rule in the streets across the country. Some would argue that a number of other - suspiciously Pagan - activities, which had previously been stamped out by Christianity, such as rolling wheels of fire down hills and torchlit processions, were subtly reintroduced as part of the Bonfire celebrations.

As the years went by, it became clear that the Fifth was getting out of control, and during the early 1800s there were successive attempts to stamp it out. However, this opposition seemed not to deter those who were by now used to having anarchistic fun in the streets at least once a year and were not keen to see it lost. Although some towns began to restrict their commemorations to bonfires and fireworks, others refused.

Quite why Lewes, of all places, was so obstinate in its determination to continue the Bonfire tradition is a mystery that has never been satisfactorily explained, but something in the contrary blood of its people ensured its continuation. Now, with only Ottery St Mary in Devon maintaining similar celebrations, Lewes has become the 'Bonfire Capital' of the world, renowned for its huge annual festival of fire - and its traditions of controversy.

After much conflict with authorities (which led to the development of the Bonfire uniform - the anonymous striped smuggler jumper - so that miscreants couldn't be easily identified), the 1850s saw the evolution of a more restrained manifestation of the Fifth with the formation of official 'Bonfire societies', with agreed territories and regulations. A century later, a 'Bonfire council' was created. Currently, seven societies exist: Lewes Borough and Cliffe (the earliest, both forming in 1853), Commercial Square, Nevill (which has its main bonfire a week before the Fifth), Southover (recently revived), South Street and Waterloo. Other societies around Sussex come into Lewes to join them for the big night of spectacle.

This book, then, is a record of what Bonfire is today, an account of what the centuries of strife and the refusal to let go of a tradition now give us for just one night of the year.

One:
Before the Fifth

As the air becomes chillier and autumn sets in, the appearance of striped shirts and effigies on Lewes streets announces the beginning of 'Bonfire' season. Meanwhile, societies around the provinces hold their pre-Fifth displays. Smoke and distant booms begin to fill the nights.

Left: Bonfire stalwart Andy Freeman of Cliffe society joins his compatriots selling Bonfire programmes at Cliffe Bridge.

Members of each Lewes Bonfire society can be seen out selling programmes and firesite tickets in the weekends before the Fifth, eager to attract passers-by to support their own activities on the night. The programmes include their schedules for the Fifth, together with articles on recent society developments and Bonfire history.

On the eve of the Fifth, society activity kicks into main gear. At the different firesites around the town (here seen at Waterloo), the towering bonfires are constructed and the frameworks for the non-mobile firework tableaux and displays are installed. These will be loaded up with their explosive components by the experts the next morning. The metal barriers which 'health and safety' now requires for bonfire displays arrive on lorries in huge stacks (see page 16) and are gradually heaved into position. A delicious air of expectancy hangs over the town.

Red paper debris from the Badge Night orgy of Chinese cracker detonations litters the street outside the Gardener's Arms.

With the firesites secured, and members on watch (lest early firebugs call), some society members gather at their 'headquarters' around the town on the eve of the Fifth for drinks and revelries. Most prominent is Cliffe's 'Badge Night', when those wishing to march the next day must attend to pick up their badges and pay their annual subs. A barely-controlled anarchy ensues in the streets

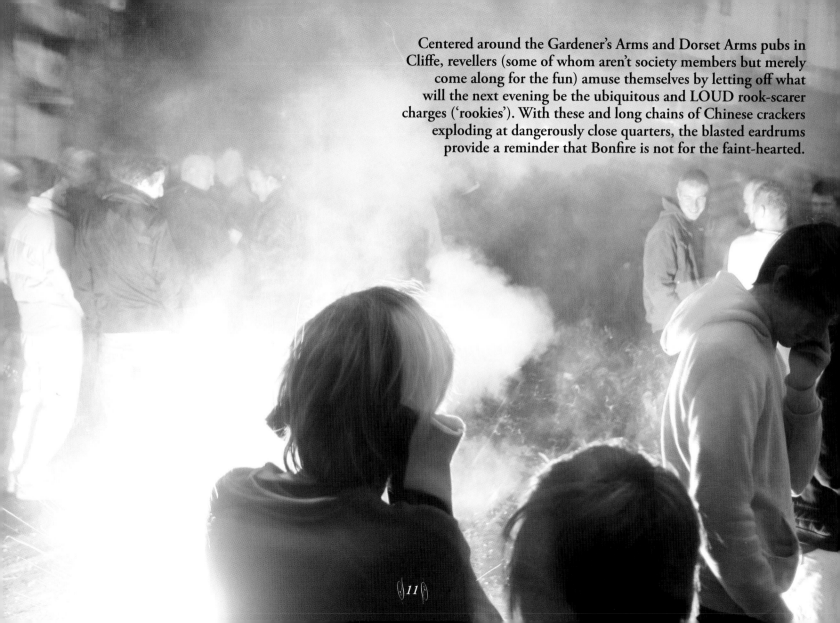

Centered around the Gardener's Arms and Dorset Arms pubs in Cliffe, revellers (some of whom aren't society members but merely come along for the fun) amuse themselves by letting off what will the next evening be the ubiquitous and LOUD rook-scarer charges ('rookies'). With these and long chains of Chinese crackers exploding at dangerously close quarters, the blasted eardrums provide a reminder that Bonfire is not for the faint-hearted.

The most controversial aspect of Lewes Bonfire first makes itself known on Badge Night. As rookies and beer distract those further up Cliffe High Street, the serious business of erecting the Cliffe society banners occupies workmen on hydraulic lifters, while curious crowds watch, mesmerised.

The banner slogans uphold the tradition of Bonfire's traumatic religious origins. Each year, the 'No Popery' controversy makes headlines, and each year the Cliffe society digs its heels in a little further on the issue.

There is more to the banners than just the 'No Popery' entry. One simply wishes well to all Cliffe subscribers, while the other records the names of the Lewes martyrs who were burned to death during the Marian persecutions of the mid-1500s - see pages 24-25.

The most controversial of the banners by day. The tradition of the anti-Papist banners derives from what the Pope represented at the time of the 1605 Gunpowder Plot - foreign tyranny and oppression. Cliffe members maintain that it is not aimed at modern Catholicism, and most Lewesians accept this as a given. (This issue is explored more fully on pages 46-47.)

The morning of the Fifth dawns to the sight of the banners in their full glory over Cliffe High Street, while the red cracker paper puzzles those unaware of what occurred there the night before.

IN MEMORY OF

DIRICK CARVER
THOMAS HARLAND
JOHN OSWALD
THOMAS AVINGTON
THOMAS REED
THOMAS WOOD
THOMAS MYLES
RICHARD WOODMAN
GEORGE STEVENS

ALEXANDER HOSMAN
WILLIAM MAINARD
THOMASINA WOOD
MARGERY MORRIS
JAMES MORRIS
DENIS BURGES
ANN ASHDON
MARY GROVES

PROTESTANT MARTYRS OF LEWES
1555 - 1557
"FAITHFUL UNTO DEATH"

DESIGNED BY ERNEST JR
DESMOND MOORE

NO
POPERY

BEST WISHES
TO CLIFFE
SUBSCRIBERS

Two:
The Fifth

It's the morning of the Fifth at last. An air of anticipation is felt across the town. The streets busy with workmen boarding up shop windows to ward off the crush of the crowds, which will fill the streets just hours later. Metal barriers are unloaded from lorries and speaker systems are erected.

SECURITY
GROUP
01273
680056

57

HOTEL

AUCTIONEERS
&
ESTATE AGENTS

White
Hart
Hotel

P

KINGS FRAMERS

REMEMBER
REMEMBER

SPECIALIST
GLASSES
••
U.V.
REFLECTIVE
••
ANTI-GLARE
••
MIRRORS
••
DRY
MOUNTING
••
HAND
PAINTED FRAMES
••
CONSULTANCY
SERVICE

Left: One shop protects itself to the point of obscuring its name. The place where people have to pay their parking fines allows no chances for opportunistic reprisals..!

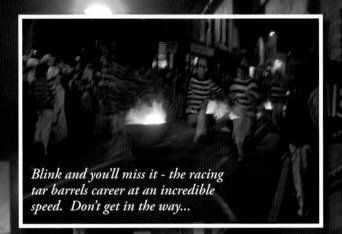

Blink and you'll miss it - the racing tar barrels career at an incredible speed. Don't get in the way...

Around 4.30pm, the central streets of Lewes are barred to traffic and the activities of the Bonfire societies take over the town, for one night only. Police clear the way as men and women in striped jumpers and elaborate costumes can be seen hurrying to their respective society headquarters. The first processions begin to take place. The sounds of marching bands float across the town from all directions, while echoing booms announce that the Fifth is properly under way. Cliffe begins its traditions around 6.00pm with the racing of blazing barrels along Cliffe High Street (right), first the ladies, and then the men.

Early processions begin as marchers follow their traditional routes (see page 26). Some societies share 'territories', such as Cliffe and South Street (seen here), which both use Cliffe High Street as their main parading ground.

Between 6.00pm and 7.30pm, each Bonfire society makes its way one by one to pay tribute to the most solemn and affecting part of the Fifth - the remembrance ceremonies at the High Street's central War Memorial. Firework poppies and burning crosses are lit to pay respects to those Lewes residents who fell in the wars of the last century and any since. A period of silence (broken only by the ignorant) is held and *The Last Post* is played by each society band in turn; always a moving moment.

'Lest We Forget' has a double-meaning in Lewes, referring both to the war dead, and to the origins of Bonfire itself.

LEST WE FORGET

The Meaning of the Crosses

People new to Lewes Bonfire Night are sometimes shocked or confused by the recurring motif of the burning cross. Contrary to the occasional tabloid nonsense, which has been known to crazily suggest Satanic or Ku Klux Klan connotations, the crosses have a more heartfelt and complex meaning here. At the War Memorial they serve as a reminder of the thousands of crosses which mark the war cemetries across Europe, but they also symbolise the fiery strength of religious feeling which began Bonfire, as well as commemorating the Lewes martyrs (see over).

Exploding firework crosses are a mark of respect for the war dead, not a controversy. The groups of seventeen fiery cruciforms which are paraded through the streets represent the seventeen protestant martyrs who died not far from the spot of today's War Memorial during the Marian persecutions of the mid-1500s.

The Lewes Martyrs

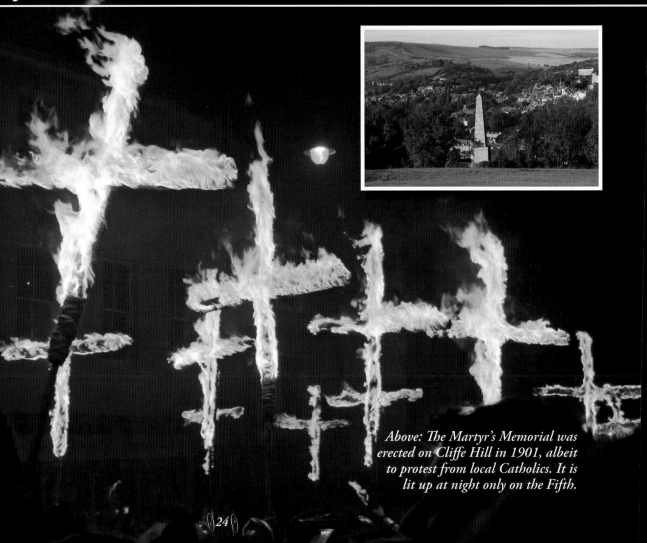

Between 1555 and 1557, Queen Mary's brief succession to the throne (after her father Henry VIII) saw a disastrous attempt to restore Britain to Catholicism after the Protestant Reformation which had turned the country upside down in the decades before. Refusing to recant their Protestantism, which they believed must surely have been inspired by God, martyrs around the country went to the flame rather than submit once more to the rule of Rome. In Lewes, seventeen Protestants, including women, were burnt at the stake outside the old Star Inn (site of today's Town Hall) during that period. Mary's early death ended the Catholic revival.

Above: The Martyr's Memorial was erected on Cliffe Hill in 1901, albeit to protest from local Catholics. It is lit up at night only on the Fifth.

IN MEMORY OF

DIRICK CARVER
THOMAS HARLAND
JOHN OSWALD
THOMAS AVINGTON
THOMAS REED
THOMAS WOOD
THOMAS MYLES
RICHARD WOODMAN
GEORGE STEVENS

ALEXANDER HOSMAN
WILLIAM MAINARD
THOMASINA WOOD
MARGERY MORRIS
JAMES MORRIS
DENIS BURGES
ANN ASHDON
MARY GROVES

PROTESTANT MARTYRS OF LEWES
1555 - 1557
"FAITHFUL UNTO DEATH"

PRESENTED IN MEMORY OF
DESMOND MOORE

Cliffe's banner, which remembers the names of the Lewes martyrs. Despite its long resonance within local history, the commemoration of the martyrs on the Fifth is a relatively new addition to the Bonfire celebrations, having grown in the early 1900s. But it is entirely in keeping with the depth of the religious tradition which makes Lewes Bonfire more than just an empty pageant.

Moving on from the War Memorial ceremonies, processions continue as traditional parts of the town are covered by different societies. In earlier centuries, clashes between rival Bonfire groups became heated and rowdy, but the formation of the societies and co-operation between them during the 1800s streamlined the order of the Fifth. Now parades throughout the night follow set established patterns in defined territories across Lewes, each society respecting the others and waiting in turn if the same streets need to be traversed

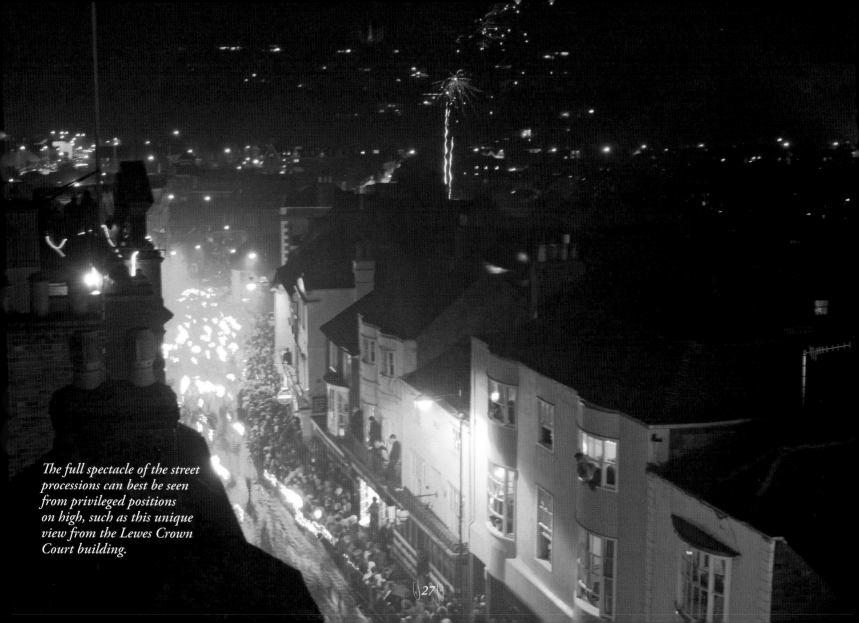

The full spectacle of the street processions can best be seen from privileged positions on high, such as this unique view from the Lewes Crown Court building.

Vendors and Stalls

With thousands upon thousands of visitors descending on Lewes for the night (not necessarily welcomed by the societies, who insist, verbally at least, that Bonfire is for locals alone), inevitably the streets are filled with novelty vendors and refreshment stalls.

In more recent years, the number and behaviour of vendors has become far more regulated, with most of the burger and hot dog vans banished to the car park behind Friar's Walk. Past decades saw vendors creating havoc - and leaving piles of rubbish - by setting up on any kerbside or verge. Now cordons and heavier policing prevent this, leaving the streets to the societies and public alone.

No Fifth would be complete without the fluorescent glowing toys beloved by children and young adults alike. Light-sabre fights often break out on Bonfire Night.

Some High Street cafes risk the crush and leave the boards off, capitalising on the busiest night of the year.

Cliffe Bridge

For a number of societies, including Cliffe, Borough and South Street, the picturesque Cliffe Bridge over the River Ouse acts as a central focus for many of the activities. The tar barrel races (page 18) begin from here, an effigy of the Martyrs' Memorial (page 24) is ignited on it and the seventeen martyr crosses are also plunged into the river here - as are burning barrels, commemorating clashes which once supposedly took place on the bridge between rival societies in years long past. In this new era of 'health and safety', however, the public are increasingly kept off the bridge itself.

A blazing barrel tips into the Ouse. These moments are over in a literal flash, but are still worth catching - if you can get a view of them from within the heaving crowds.

The evocative sight of a procession over Cliffe Bridge, as seen from the Eastgate Street car park. Going off the beaten track can provide unexpected perspectives on Bonfire and little quiet moments of reflection.

Policing Bonfire

The Lewes celebrations, of course, have a long history of clashing with authority. Although the obvious failure of the many historical attempts to stamp out Bonfire (page 4) has now been conceded, a feeling still pervades that the emergency services and police would be much happier if it were all to stop. The appearance of riot squads on one Fifth some years ago nearly caused a riot in itself, a mistake not repeated since, but in a society of ever-more draconian controls and surveillance, how long the freedom of the streets will be granted in the current way remains to be seen. In addition, the cost of policing Bonfire - and who pays - has also become an issue in more recent times.

The most ubiquitous sight of the Fifth, beyond the many striped jumpers, is that of the yellow-jacketed police. With thousands of people in the streets, order must be maintained, and many officers do well in maintaining a good humour to match the mood of the night. However, there have been concerns in more recent years that the policing has become too heavy and threatening, even leading to effigies of protest being paraded (*right*).

Despite concerns about the forcefulness of Bonfire policing, few would deny that officers sometimes have a challenging task in the face of fire, rookies and alcohol, and the majority rise to the occasion well.

Guy Fawkes

Below: A Fawkes effigy stored in the dungeons of Commerical Square society, condemned forever, in Lewes at least, to literally be the 'fall guy'.

Guido Fawkes Traitor

Another common feature of processions on the Fifth, predictably enough, is the paraded figure of Guy Fawkes himself. Although just one conspirator amongst several in 1605, it is the shortened name of Guido Fawkes that has stuck in the national psyche, an ever-demonised symbol of threats to English sovereignty. Unlucky enough to be the one caught amongst the gunpowder barrels beneath Parliament, his torture and agonising execution - hung, drawn and quartered (not burned) - along with fellow plotters, served as a warning to any other potential champions of Roman Catholicism. Controversial recent evidence suggests the Gunpowder Plotters may even have been deliberately set up by the Protestant government as a way of inciting further hatred towards Rome, but in Lewes such caveats hold no weight - Fawkes will always carry the guilt.

One irony of Bonfire, never entirely squared, is that it has come to represent stands against authority - and yet Guy Fawkes, who did exactly that in times of his faith's oppression, is condemned for it on the Fifth and the preservation of the status quo is celebrated... Defenders counter that Fawkes is an exception because he was trying to give away home rule to a foreign power. Debates will doubtless continue for a long time yet.

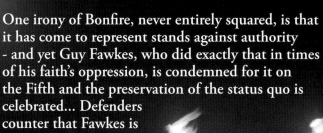

REMEMBER, REMEMBER

Remember, remember the Fifth of November
The Gunpowder Treason and plot
I see no reason why Gunpowder Treason
Should ever be forgot

Guy Fawkes, Guy Fawkes, 'twas his intent
To blow up the King and the Parliament
Three score barrels of powder below
Poor old England to overthrow

By God's providence he was catch'd
With a dark lantern and burning match
Holler boys, holler boys, ring bells ring
Holler boys, holler boys, God Save the King!

TRADITIONAL

Midway through the evening, many of the Bonfire societies (though not all - Cliffe, for instance, notably abstains), including those from other Sussex towns and villages, gather together into a huge parade known as the 'Grand Procession'. Its presence fills the long route from Western Road, down the High Street to Library Corner, and can take an hour to pass. It's here where the dedication of the societies really shows, as a myriad of costumes and effigies rolls endlessly past, punctuated by the rousing music of the many brass bands, drummers and morris men, all marching with determination

The blazing torches and drawn barrels make for an impressive sight - and offer welcome heat on cold Fifths.

Rookies explode in burning barrel carts as crowds flinch away, scared, amused and fascinated all at the same time by the delicious insanity of Bonfire.

In the High Street near the imposing Crown Court buildings, mobile fireworks or smaller effigies are ignited to cheering crowds. Incredibly, in olden days, when roads were much narrower than today and many buildings were made from wood, societies held their main bonfires and displays in the streets. A series of devastating fires eventually saw these moved to safer sites.

With rookies exploding at close quarters, and flares and flaming torches being brandished at head height, the Bonfire experience can be unsettling for the nervous. With the crush of people behind barriers and all the minus points of being in a crowd, it isn't ideal for young children either. Each year someone will complain to the press about the noise and danger, to which, reasonably enough, the society answer is - don't come, then!

Morris men dance as the red flares which illuminate so much of the Fifth burn brightly

Bonfire Costumes

Society members who choose costumes above the smuggler stripes spend many hours in the run-up to the Fifth perfecting their generally very authentic looks. A special costume competition is also held in the Town Hall each year. Every style, including Zulus, Romans, Pearly Kings and Queens, Tudor folk and Vikings can be seen.

A US Civil War soldier plays with fire, while South American warriors risk their feathers.

41

Street Theatre

As well as the amazing costumes and livery, societies are not above using props to enhance the inherent theatre of Bonfire Night. The old hand-drawn Lewes fire cart, with its cohort of Victorian firemen, always makes an appearance for instance (*left*), while Native Americans (that's still 'Red Indians' to most marchers) and cowboys ignite a totem pole in the streets (*below*). The Viking warriors and womenfolk, meanwhile, actually have their own longboat to take through the streets (*below left and opposite*); always an impressive sight.

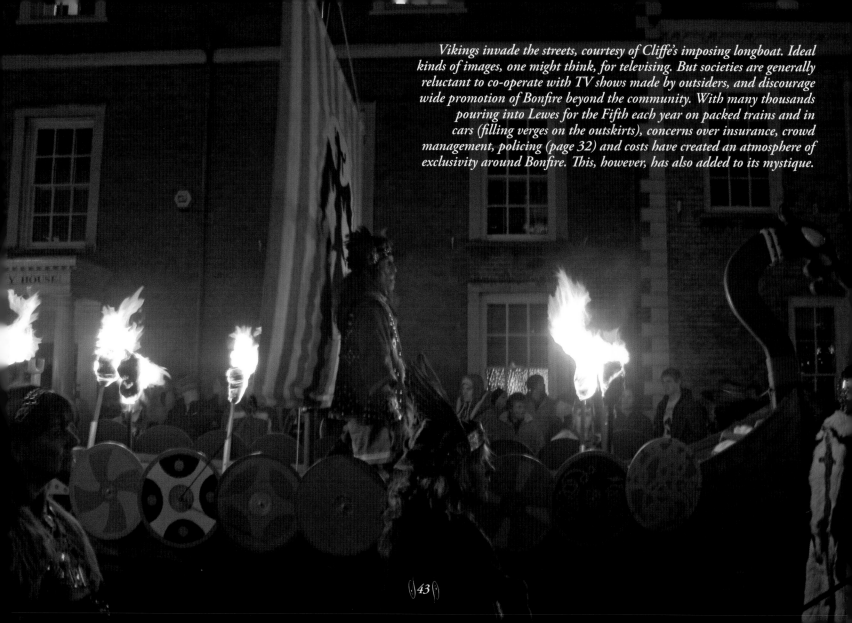

Vikings invade the streets, courtesy of Cliffe's imposing longboat. Ideal kinds of images, one might think, for televising. But societies are generally reluctant to co-operate with TV shows made by outsiders, and discourage wide promotion of Bonfire beyond the community. With many thousands pouring into Lewes for the Fifth each year on packed trains and in cars (filling verges on the outskirts), concerns over insurance, crowd management, policing (page 32) and costs have created an atmosphere of exclusivity around Bonfire. This, however, has also added to its mystique.

Parading the Tableaux

Although large displays are no longer allowed in the streets for obvious safety reasons, some societies, notably Cliffe and Commercial Square, still parade their main firework tableaux in their processions to the firesites - to cheers and jeers from the crowds, depending on the target. Usually grotesque caricatures of global politicians who have annoyed or concerned the societies in some way, or large symbolic references to some looming local issue, their towering presence over the crowds never fails to impress. If anyone ever thought Condoleezza Rice was a scary woman, this particular year's Cliffe effigy, seen here, would leave them in little doubt. The subjects of each year's tableaux are much-guarded secrets, chosen behind closed doors by society hierarchies. Constructed in concealed sheds at unknown locations, the results are revealed only on the Fifth, a surprise even to most of the memberships. Unlocking the puzzle of exactly what point is being made by the sometimes enigmatic tableaux is part of the fun.

Rear of the year... Bonfire style.

Guy Fawkes himself, of course, is never far behind any other figure of derision being hauled through the crowds.

Irreverence is a key part of Bonfire. Here, the rear of the policeman effigy seen on page 32 reveals a Bonfire Boy about to make things go with a bang... Other victims of society humour, usually offending local dignitaries or politicians, may find their heads on pikes as 'Enemies of Bonfire'.

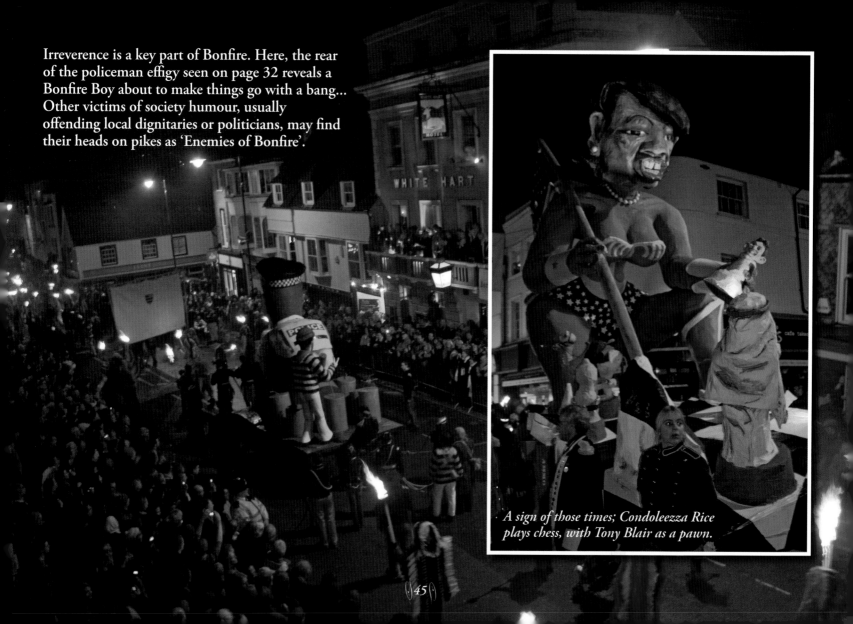

A sign of those times; Condoleezza Rice plays chess, with Tony Blair as a pawn.

The Papal Effigy

The 'No Popery' banners across Cliffe High Street already give away the big shock value of Lewes Bonfire, but the appearance of the Papal effigy in the Cliffe procession is still a breathtaking moment of controversy for newcomers. Society members insist that it represents Pope Paul V of 1605 alone, the symbolic inspiration behind the Gunpowder Plot, and not the current incumbent of the Vatican. However, each year yet another contrived tabloid scandal or a recently moved-in and offended Lewes resident attempts to have the effigy banned - to no avail. In a rapidly changing world, tradition is sometimes all people have to anchor themselves, and many Lewesians feel that once one link to history is eroded, down will come all the others. What outsiders fail to see, they hold, is that the Pope being paraded is a symbol of oppression and control; something always to be fought, no matter from which direction it comes. For the purposes of Bonfire, the Pope and Fawkes must carry the burden.

A PENNY LOAF

A penny loaf to feed old Pope
A farthing cheese to choke him
A pint of beer to rinse it down
A faggot of sticks to burn him

Burn him in a tub of tar
Burn him like a blazing star
Burn his body from his head
Then we'll say old Pope is dead

Hip Hip Hoorah!
Hip Hip Hoorah!
Hip Hip Hoorah!

TRADITIONAL

Some have tried to draw links between Lewes Bonfire and the Orange parades in Northern Ireland. Although the Protestant bias of the Fifth is made clear in Cliffe's banners commemorating the 1688 landing (on another 5th November) of William of Orange on English soil to see off the threat of the Catholic sympathiser King James II, the mood of it all in Lewes is very different - light tradition, not ingrained conflict.

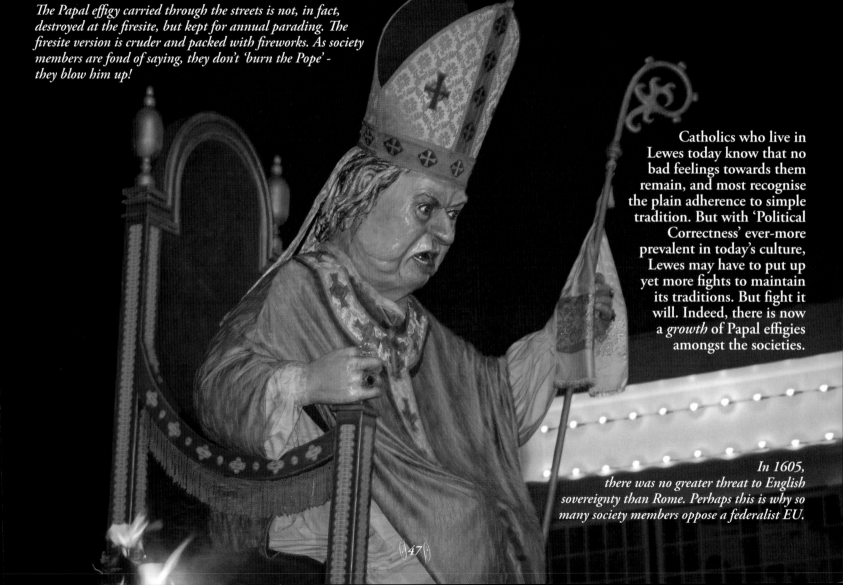

The Papal effigy carried through the streets is not, in fact, destroyed at the firesite, but kept for annual parading. The firesite version is cruder and packed with fireworks. As society members are fond of saying, they don't 'burn the Pope' - they blow him up!

Catholics who live in Lewes today know that no bad feelings towards them remain, and most recognise the plain adherence to simple tradition. But with 'Political Correctness' ever-more prevalent in today's culture, Lewes may have to put up yet more fights to maintain its traditions. But fight it will. Indeed, there is now a *growth* of Papal effigies amongst the societies.

In 1605, there was no greater threat to English sovereignty than Rome. Perhaps this is why so many society members oppose a federalist EU.

Those with access to houses and offices overlooking the High Street have an obvious advantage to those crammed down below in the streets. Sometimes perilously perched on narrow ledges and balconies, the risk is deemed worth it by the onlookers as it affords such an impressive overview of the scale of events - something not always easy to grasp in the crowds.

One visit to Lewes Bonfire is not enough to take in the totality of the many different events occurring across the town, and people don't always realise that there are six separate societies doing different things simultaneously. Indeed, it can take several years of visits to Lewes on the Fifth to see all the varied things it has to offer. But from the rooftops, especially as the earlier firework displays begin and processions are still in progress, at least some sense of its hugeness can be absorbed.

A generally good-natured game of one-upmanship can occur as those with the advantage of balconies above goad those down below, stuck in attempting to move through very crushed crowds, negotiating barriers and unforgiving policemen. Those above will always win though, so it's best to concede with laughter - don't forget, drinks can easily be tipped downwards.

A Pause Before the Fires

With the earlier parts of the Fifth's rituals dealt with, the societies
begin to gather themselves for their own 'Grand' processions to the
firesites, where the climax - though not the end - of the evening occurs.
Barrels burn as old torches are gathered and people warm themselves
around them. There is a brief lull and a sense of waiting.

Cliffe society begins its procession to its firesite, with a typically defiant slogan in Sussex dialect. 'We wunt be druv' - i.e. driven from the streets - sums up much of the Bonfire ethos. Love it or hate it, Lewes Bonfire is here to stay. Only in times of extreme crisis has the Fifth ever been cancelled or postponed; during the two World Wars, for instance, or because of severe flooding. Simple rain, however, never stops play. The processions and fires go on, even in downpours and damp costumes.

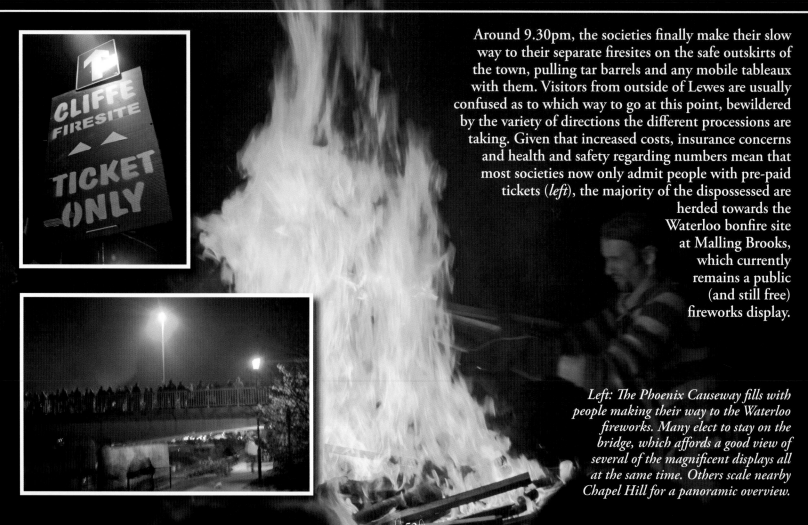

Around 9.30pm, the societies finally make their slow way to their separate firesites on the safe outskirts of the town, pulling tar barrels and any mobile tableaux with them. Visitors from outside of Lewes are usually confused as to which way to go at this point, bewildered by the variety of directions the different processions are taking. Given that increased costs, insurance concerns and health and safety regarding numbers mean that most societies now only admit people with pre-paid tickets (*left*), the majority of the dispossessed are herded towards the Waterloo bonfire site at Malling Brooks, which currently remains a public (and still free) fireworks display.

Left: The Phoenix Causeway fills with people making their way to the Waterloo fireworks. Many elect to stay on the bridge, which affords a good view of several of the magnificent displays all at the same time. Others scale nearby Chapel Hill for a panoramic overview.

The bonfires are usually already ablaze by the time the societies arrive at their firesites. They provide very welcome respite from the cold wait amongst spectators in the muddy fields.

At the Firesites

With the recent revival of Southover Bonfire Society, there are now
six bonfires and displays across Lewes on the Fifth. The air across the
town is filled with smoke, sulphur and the pervading tinge of paraffin.
Environmentalists, inevitably, have long raised objections, but there's no
denying the unique nostalgic atmosphere created by the smell of the Fifth.

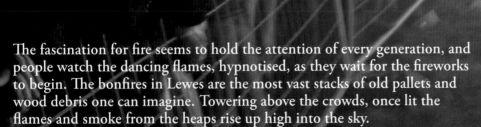

The fascination for fire seems to hold the attention of every generation, and
people watch the dancing flames, hypnotised, as they wait for the fireworks
to begin. The bonfires in Lewes are the most vast stacks of old pallets and
wood debris one can imagine. Towering above the crowds, once lit the
flames and smoke from the heaps rise up high into the sky.

In addition to the large society events, there are, of course, many smaller fires and mini-displays taking place in gardens across the town. The sky rockets from private parties keep the waiting masses distracted before the 'big guns' begin.

Ancient Resonance?

The eternal draw to fire and the seemingly Pagan connotations of Bonfire, for all its Christian roots, have been noted by many observers. Although it is hard to specifically pin down a direct thread leading to the distant past, it's hard to deny the resonance of some of the old fire rituals with what goes on today. Race memory, or simple coincidence?

Right: Like a scene from the Western Front, figures wait in the mist and smoke for the main fireworks to begin.

There is evidence to suggest that Lewes may have been an important pre-Roman ritual site. Some believe many of the banned Pagan traditions were quietly sneaked back into the ritual year under the cover of Bonfire Night.

The Clergymen's Charges

The Christian origins of modern Bonfire are soon reasserted with the arrival on the platforms of 'clergymen', who (largely unintelligibly in the cold autumn breeze) proceed to bellow the charges of treason laid against Guy Fawkes. For those who can hear, the traditional call of 'What shall we do with him?' is met with the mob response 'Burn him!'. Neither burned, nor killed as horribly as he was in real life, Fawkes is instead promptly exploded.

The burning crosses often make a reappearance at this stage in the evening, as the roots of religious strife come to the fore once again.

As the clergymen go through their routine, usually to
jeering crowds anxious for the explosions to start, rookies
and other fireworks are traditionally thrown at them at
dangerously close quarters. For all its religious origins,
there's not much respect for the men in robes. Ear-plugs
and eye-protectors are recommended for this job.

Fireworks

At last, the tableaux are ignited and sky rockets fired. If the timing is right, the downland around Lewes echoes with the deep booms from the often simultaneous displays lighting up the sky on every horizon, silhouetting the rooftops and towers of the old town.

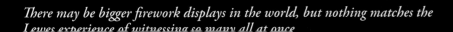

There may be bigger firework displays in the world, but nothing matches the Lewes experience of witnessing so many all at once.

Be they male or female, old or young, the respectable or the inevitable drunken yob, everyone stops to watch the dazzling show before them. Fireworks remain a unique entertainment, their power unrivalled.

After the Fire

In most places, the climax of the fireworks display would be the end of the evening's proceedings - but not in Lewes. There is just a brief time for warming hands around the embers and watching the curious life-like behaviour of sparks and flames in the now much-reduced bonfires, before the societies set off again, back into the town to head for their respective headquarters to enjoy the less organised revelries which will truly end the evening.

It is true that the majority of spectators from outside of the town head home after the bonfires and displays, huddling in the crammed queues at the train station or trudging out to cars abandoned on the far outskirts of the traffic-ban zone. But those who want the full Bonfire experience stay a while longer yet...

Scenes like this have barely changed throughout the centuries of Bonfire, except that by all accounts the earlier years were even more rowdy and dangerous than what we still have today.

With the more public face of Bonfire now done, society members relax into a more informal - and more anarchistic - mode at their headquarters across the town, seen here at Commercial Square's titular site; ironically, directly outside the Police Station. Small bonfires of torch debris are lit in the streets. Ear-splitting rookies are cast into the flames and the more adventurous leap across them, now inspired greatly, of course, by 'Dutch courage'.

Commercial Square society, with the handy balcony provided by the rise of houses overlooking the square (*left*), have traditionally conducted savagely honest and hilarious 'sermons' on current events, courtesy of the late leading 'clergyman' Paul Wheeler (seen here in red, top left), who tragically died in a road accident in 2008. The society have vowed to continue the tradition.

The traditional 'Bonfire Prayers' - *Remember, Remember* (page 35) and *A Penny Loaf* (page 46) are also recited here and across the town with great gusto.

Eruptions of Chinese crackers do all they can to disrupt the balcony sermon. All part of the entertaining madness of Bonfire.

Paul Wheeler's loss to Bonfire was huge, and he will be greatly remembered for many years by Lewesians and society members alike.

As the very last post-midnight processions come to
a close, a kind of pyrotechnic free-for-all erupts in
the streets, as remaining stocks of Chinese crackers,
Roman Candles and rookies are exploded in a final
frenzy. Once, this kind of thing would occur during
the main processions, with fireworks liberally thrown
into the crowds. Later regulations - and sheer common
sense - have relegated these activities to the late-shift.

These images sum up the Lewes Bonfire experience; noisy, insane and glorious. In a climate of increased state nannying, how long it will be allowed to continue in this way is another matter, but Lewes certainly won't go down without a fight.

Order Restored

Now Bonfire Boys and Girls, together with the last spectators, slowly make their way home, relinquishing the temporary grip of power they have had on the town for their one night of the year. Signs of the usual order make themselves known, as ambulances ferry the inevitable minor casualties, and the police reassert themselves, vans tearing down the High Street at crazy speeds.

Embers smoulder in quiet corners, as the streets grow increasingly deserted. The Fifth is over for another year and Lewes returns to its usual state as a respectable Sussex town. Well, nearly.

Three:
After the Fifth

The Morning

The morning after the Fifth
is like piecing together a lost
dream. The overnight street
cleaners do their work well.
A few fragments and tell-tale
signs of what occurred just
hours before remain for a
while, but soon all traces are
cleared away. Responsibility
for the odd unplanned damage
(*post box, above*) is sorted
out, hangovers recede and life
restores itself to normal.

Above: Almost as if it never happened; the High Street next day. An army of overtime-paid council workers do their best to restore clean streets in the early hours, but happily a few nostalgic traces always remain in the morning sunshine.

As the flattened charcoal of the previous night's towering infernos gasp their last puffs of smoke, and the odd striped Bonfire Boy or Girl makes their way into town for final clear-ups and hair-of-the-dog debriefings, the unique smell of the Fifth still hangs in the air as a last reminder.

The Countdown Begins

Lewes Bonfire Night has a magic to it that is unique and compelling. Always likely to remain controversial, its challenges to authority will doubtless go on, especially if there are renewed attempts to dampen its spirit, either through legalities or the insidious creep of insurance technicalities. In a world that seems increasingly keen to curtail freedom of thought and speech in the name of our 'protection', Bonfire is a timely reminder that real security comes from celebrating liberty and remembering times when oppression has threatened it. Long may the spirit of Lewes and Bonfire live on.

The spent tubes that provided such spectacle the night before rest innocently in the morning sun, their job done. For those in this curious and fascinating town for whom Bonfire is in the blood, be they society member or spectator, this is not the end, of course - simply the beginning of the countdown to do it all again in 364 days time.